Narcissism

Learning To Find Peace Following A Toxic Relationship With Psychopaths And Antisocial

(Abuse That Is Emotional And Narcissistic)

Jordan Mercer

TABLE OF CONTENT

Gas Lighting And Humiliation Tactics 1

Overt Versus Hidden Narcissism 20

Couples 30

Relationship Based On Narcissism 40

The Narcissist's True Self Is The False Self. 57

Narcissist Mothers 94

Daughters Of Narcissistic Mothers Are Prone To Develop Narcissistic Tendencies 118

Can A Narcissistic Family Transform? 130

What Are Narcissism And Narcissistic Personality Disorder? 146

Gas Lighting And Humiliation Tactics

What is the origin of the term gaslighting, and what is it? The term gaslighting was derived from the film Gaslight. In the film, the spouse repeatedly turns on and off the old gaslight. And when his wife inquires as to who is turning the light on and off, he denies the occurrence. The wife gradually begins to question her own reality. Then she loses touch with reality. Eventually, she becomes deranged. Whether intentional or not, denying someone's reality is gaslighting.

Gaslighting is a type of psychological mistreatment. It occurs when person A questions the veracity of person B, leaving person B bewildered. This type of behavior is characteristic of narcissists, who engage in it to protect their fragile egos. Throughout this process, the narcissist disregards how much their denial and gaslighting tactics harm others.

Gaslighting is a manipulative and emotionally abusive technique. When a companion is subjected to second-guessing about their own reality, it is frustrating for that partner. They believe they are losing control of the universe and possibly going insane. There are numerous covert indicators that can help you identify someone who is gaslighting you. Pay close attention when you hear the following:

You are not permitted to feel that way.

-It appears that you are exaggerating. -I regret that you have chosen to make yourself feel this way.

Why are you unable to let go of the past?

-You are overreacting -No one will ever love you as much as I do -You are overly dramatic -That never occurred You should not feel this way -I believe you are mentally ill -You require assistance -Why can't you get a job?

Stop acting like a victim. Why are you always so angry?

When someone says such things, they invalidate your feelings and experiences. These statements are laden with a cloud of condemnation, as if you have no right to feel; this is dehumanizing. It removes a person's humanity and natural capacity to empathize. It would be like informing someone they are hungry when they are obviously not hungry. Imagine telling someone that they are fatigued when they actually feel well-rested.

When confronted with such remarks, the best course of action is to withdraw from the conversation because you cannot prevail. Even if you mechanically express your emotions, the narcissist will continue to gaslight you and will not have empathy for the emotions you are experiencing. They will continue to manipulate and distort your words, thereby increasing their mistreatment of you. Avoid conflict at all costs because you will achieve nothing.

Deflection is another indicator that your companion or someone else is gaslighting you. A deflection is a form of gaslighting, and it occurs when you want to discuss something significant for the relationship's improvement. As soon as you begin to express concerns, your narcissists immediately change the subject. While you are being reasonable and discussing a current issue, they deflect and bring up a past issue or something irrelevant. The problem with deflection is that it creates a situation in which you appear bad and are at fault.

If you find yourself in an argument where you must bring the other individual back to the topic at hand, the conversation is over. Due to their avoidance responses, you may be forced to accept the possibility that you will not have the conversation. The third type of gaslighting occurs when a person utterly denies your perception of reality. They will assert that the event never occurred.

When we are informed that something never occurred, we have a tendency to question our memories and retrace our steps. When confronted with evidence that something did occur and the truth, the narcissist will respond with wrath or deflection. Narcissists dislike having the inconsistencies of their gaslighting exposed. When you feel compelled to record your conversations or compose a letter or email, this is a clear indication that you are being gaslighted.

You may believe that if you express your feelings and concerns in writing, the narcissist will understand because there are no interruptions and they will attend. This is false. Narcissists do not heed. You spend days and weekends writing or pondering the ideal way to express yourself, but once you do, their responses become even more offensive. They will turn the tables on you.

The easiest method to handle such situations is to end the conversation since you are not going anywhere. All of these behaviors are detrimental for humans to engage in. Constantly having to justify and defend oneself is beyond exhausting. This entire procedure is comparable to a twisted mind game that is detrimental to your mental health and sanity. You do need professional assistance and resources to manage with and recover from emotional abuse.

You may believe that the narcissist is aware of their actions. And the answer is difficult because some individuals may be aware of their behaviors and patterns while others are unaware. Due to their fundamental insecurity, narcissists are singularly concentrated and motivated to defend their reality and their interpretation of events. They are in defensive mode and are actively contemplating manipulating you. Instead, they lack empathy, which prevents them from considering how their actions affect their loved ones. Therefore, the narcissist believes that they have the right to do it. And the fact that they are vulnerable indicates that they do not wish to be discovered and exposed.

This explains why narcissists are defensive and attempt to shield what they perceive as a failure or error. They use gaslighting to avoid unsettling situations. Because they do not want to cope with your emotions and experiences, they minimize them. The minimization is a passive form of gaslighting, which makes it more dangerous because they do it without considering.

In the process of denying and downplaying a person's emotions or reality over time, the gaslighted individual experiences overwhelming self-doubt. Being in such a relationship is toxic and detrimental to your emotional and mental health. If you are at the point in your relationship where you question whether there is something wrong with you for bringing up a subject, this is a clear indication that your relationship is toxic.

As you live in dread of not being able to communicate your needs or emotions, you are simultaneously becoming invisible and losing your sense of self. Your self-esteem is deteriorating, and you are neglecting yourself. And what maintains you in the game for the long haul are the promises of change and the times when it appears that your partner is making progress. A hopeful disposition will keep you in the game for the long haul, and you will eventually repair or assist them in changing. But until the narcissist seeks assistance, nothing will change.

How can someone on the receiving end of gaslighting mitigate some of the anguish and turmoil? Accept that some issues and situations will remain unresolved if you do not engage, exit the conversation, or end the conversation. Accept the actuality and true condition of your narcissistic partner and the nature of your relationship. Seek assistance and adhere to your network of support; they are your lifeline.

I was extremely anxious on race day. That year, I was hosting the National qualifier, so I had numerous responsibilities. I had delegated responsibility to our auxiliary coaches and dispersed parents throughout the course for Tess's race. She had participated in approximately five practices over the course of two weeks, but she was unable to run very far and struggled with a disability. When I attempted to settle her down and ask if she didn't want to do this, she responded that she was fine with it. I had called Melanie to inquire if she would attend the race. As of her response, she was at the gym. Obviously, Rock was standing next to her. She informed me that she would not be attending because she had other obligations.

She was vague, but it was clear she had plans to go out. This weekend, I was with my children, but this day was monumental.

Each age group's best two teams and top thirty finishers qualified for Nationals. The 12-and-under division was the final race of the day. At the race, there were participants from all over New York State. I was anxious and enthusiastic for Tess.

On a typical race weekend, participants will depart immediately following their race, but not today. It was widely known that my daughter had suffered a stroke earlier in the year. Other coaches and parents frequently inquired about her recovery progress. The running community is fantastic in this regard. They embrace all people. Thus, when the 12 & Under race began, the venue was still crowded with runners from other events. I counted thirty competitors at the starting line without knowing the final tally. The gun was fired, and the runners ran away. 150 meters into the race, Tess was one hundred meters behind the leader. However, there she went, limping along. I had my phone on me and had requested that her parents text me when she passed through their checkpoint. Slowly, messages began to arrive. When the winner passed the finish line, she was in the back fields. The spectators were not permitted on the backfields. Due to the presence of spotters along the course, I was exempt from the requirement to wear a helmet. Unbeknownst to me, the back fields of the race were lined with runners and parents from all the other organizations applauding for Tess. About fifty meters separated me from the finish line. My daughter would emerge from the woods with 600 meters remaining. What I observed moved me to tears. She had emerged from the forest, and thirty meters behind her, the entire group of children from previous races were jogging and applauding for her. The most significant moment of my coaching career was witnessing children of various cultures and ethnicities unite in support of a single individual. As she approached the final straightaway, she was beaming. The crowd stopped but continued to applaud as she crossed the finish line in last place but as a national qualifier!!!

I embraced her while holding back sobs. She gazed up and exclaimed, "I did it!" surely, you did, honey, surely you did. We called Melanie while driving home. She was thrilled for Tess, but it was clear that she did not comprehend the gravity of the situation. She and Rock were in the eastern region of wineries. She could not speak for very long. Tess inquired as we hung up whether Mom was okay. I informed her that Mommy had obligations today. Before we began speaking, I suggested that we order pizza and celebrate.

Two weeks later, we traveled to South Carolina for the Cross-Country National Championships. Tess had not trained extensively in the two weeks preceding Nationals. Due to post-race soreness, she only trained twice.

She was ecstatic to attend Nationals.

I asked Melanie if she planned to attend. She stated that she would respond. A week later, she informed me that she would be passing. She was unable to leave work. She declined my offer for her to depart on Friday evening. Melanie and Rock had made arrangements. It was out of character for Melanie, who was always focused on her children. How could Melanie miss two of our daughter's most important weekends, especially after her stroke? She was in a parallel universe.

People enjoy to talk. Primarily when it involves hearsay.

It had reached me that people believed Melanie was seeing someone. She refused to concede it to me. She told me only that they were friends. I believe individuals would tell me things to gauge my response. There is nothing better than going back and admitting that you misunderstood or were furious. I did not give them anything. I was emotionally irreparably wounded by the death of my family. I've always been decent under pressure, so denying the vultures access to the carcass was simple. Melanie used to tell me that if I were on one of the 9/11 hijacked flights, I would find a means to land the aircraft. Now, I am emotionless. That emotion is extinct. It is the primary reason why none of my relationships last. It's because I'm indifferent.

I was somewhat disappointed that Melanie did not attend.

Tess had set the aim of competing at Nationals in the hospital room. She frequently discussed it, but Melanie was on cloud nine.

It was a beautiful autumn day in the south. Not excessively chilly or hot. Our organization was doing extremely well! Multiple All-Americans, two National Champions, and now my 12 & Under girls were vying for the National Title! We were secure. Our under-12 females would defeat the majority of varsity HS teams. That is how competent we were. The race began, and all but one of us left quickly. My Tess was moving forward.

At the Nationals, no one is permitted on the course. You can be present for the first 300 meters and the last 300 meters of the race. After that, the competitors were pitted against the course.

That is all.

I positioned myself approximately 250 meters from the finish line because there was a spot where the females would pass with approximately 800 meters remaining in the race, allowing me to see them run twice. As the runners passed, my first two females were in first and second place. My next two runners placed ninth and twelfth, and my fifth athlete placed twenty-sixth.

As each runner past me, I looked out into the distance and spotted Tess. There is no one in her vicinity. I let out a scream that I was certain she could hear. My voice echoed through the woods. My daughters always informed me that they could hear me at events.

Something was incorrect. While running, Tess kept glancing back. As she rounded the bend and passed me with 800 meters remaining, I shouted at her to refrain from turning around. She regarded me and exclaimed, "I'm not Last!" I turned around and saw a woman laboring approximately 100 meters behind me. I yelled back that every time she turned around she lost a step, so I would keep her informed and she was not to glance back. When she passed me again with 250 meters remaining, I informed her that she had a 70-meter advantage.

Don't turn around and go! I yelled.

As she entered the final 150 meters, a line of applauding spectators greeted her. The cheers of thousands of spectators lining the final 300 meters carried her to the finish line, where she was met by her comrades.

Everywhere there were embraces. I recall Tess embracing me and saying, "I did it." I have never been more proud.

That day, a local television station interviewed me. When they asked me what I thought, I told them that four months ago, we didn't even believe she would be here, and that this was her objective. It was an excellent narrative. Tess wished to call Melanie, but we repeatedly received her voicemail. Melanie did not return our call until later that day. In contrast, I was unhappy and began to ponder what was going on. This was not the Melanie I'd known for more than 18 years.

Overt Versus Hidden Narcissism

The only difference between covert and overt narcissists is that covert narcissists are more introverted. The overt narcissist is easily identifiable because he or she is boisterous, arrogant, indifferent to the needs of others, and constantly seeking praise.

Their actions are easily observed by others, and they appear "large" in the space. In their interactions with others, overt narcissists are more extroverted.

The term covert is frequently used to imply that a covert narcissist is devious or that their desire for prominence is less intense than that of an overt (more extroverted) narcissist. Hidden or overt narcissists navigate the world with a sense of self-importance and fantasize about success and grandeur.

Whether extroverted or introverted, both overt and covert narcissists must meet the same clinical criteria in order to be diagnosed with narcissistic personality disorder. Both individuals lack the capacity to manage their self-esteem.

Before experiencing emotional distress, many individuals have fallen victim to the deceptive behavior of a covert narcissist. It may be more accurate to state that extroverted (overt) narcissists are much easier to identify than their introverted counterparts.

CHARACTERISTICS OF A COVERT NARCISSIST

If you suspect you are interacting with a covert narcissist, there are certain patterns and characteristics to look for in your daily interactions.

Having knowledge of these characteristics may provide you with the ability to recognize and avoid potentially dangerous situations.

Significance of the Passive Self
The covert narcissist's inflated sense of self and arrogance may be less apparent than the extroverted narcissist's when interacting with others.

The latent narcissist craves prominence and acclaim, but it may appear otherwise to those around them. They may offer backhanded compliments or purposely downplay their accomplishments or skills so that others will reassure them of their competence. Both overt and covert narcissists suffer from a lack of self-awareness.

The overt narcissist will seek admiration and attention, whereas the covert narcissist will employ more inconspicuous methods to achieve the same outcomes. The covert narcissist craves constant affirmation of their abilities, skills, and accomplishments, seeking for others to satisfy this need for self-importance.

Shaming and Blaming

Shaming is a strategy employed by narcissists to maintain their sense of superiority over others. The overt (extroverted) narcissist's strategy for gaining leverage may be more obvious, such as putting you down overtly, being boorish, criticizing you, and being sarcastic.

To explain why something is your fault and not theirs, the introverted, covert narcissist may adopt a kinder approach. They may even claim to be victims of your actions or engage in emotional abuse in order to gain your sympathy and admiration. Whether overt or covert, the goal is to make the other person feel small.

Resulting in Confusion

Although not always clever, some covert narcissists enjoy creating uncertainty. In lieu of accusing or demeaning, they cause individuals to reconsider and second-guess their opinions.

The covert narcissist employs this tactic as well as others to elevate themselves and maintain control over the conversation. If they can persuade you to dispute your beliefs, they will have more opportunities to abuse and control you.

Disregard and Delayed Action
Due to their intense desire for self-importance, covert narcissists will go to any lengths to maintain the spotlight on themselves. The covert narcissist is an expert at not noticing you at all, whereas the extroverted narcissist may openly push you aside or manipulate you to accomplish their objective.

It should come as no surprise that narcissists prefer to interact with compassionate and affectionate individuals. Additionally, the covert narcissist is aware of the possibility of manipulation. They have no problem telling you that you are insignificant.

Instead of telling you directly that you are insignificant, they may reject you on a date, respond to messages or emails at the last minute, be chronically late, or never make firm commitments. There is no regard for your time or interests, making you feel insignificant, unimportant, and insignificant.

Giving with Intent
In general, narcissists are not benefactors. They find it difficult to consecrate their efforts to endeavors that do not directly benefit them. A covert narcissist may appear generous to themselves, but their generosity is motivated by the desire to receive something in return.

They take care to establish a connection that allows them to be praised for their generosity. Giving is always more about the giver's concealed narcissism than the recipients.

Insensitive to Emotions
Narcissists are awful at establishing and sustaining emotional bonds with others. Hidden narcissists are not an exception. Consequently, they are neither emotionally approachable nor receptive, despite the fact that they appear kinder and less irritating than their extroverted counterpart.

A concealed narcissist may not be flattering. Given that they are constantly focused on being elevated to maintain their sense of self-importance, it is easy to understand why a covert narcissist might find it difficult to value you. A narcissist has little regard for your skills and abilities; in fact, he or she frequently has no regard for them at all.

In a relationship with a covert narcissist, you would likely do the majority of the emotional heavy lifting, just as you would with an open narcissist. Despite the fact that the concealed appears to be more emotionally accessible, it is typically a performance designed to abuse or ultimately leave the individual feeling small through neglect, blaming, or humiliation.

Because lack of empathy is one of the core characteristics of narcissistic personality disorder, the covert narcissist will not be emotionally receptive to their spouse.

Covert narcissists exhibit passive-aggressive behavior frequently. They minimize the significance of others while emphasizing their own. In addition, they accuse, humiliate, and disregard the emotions and requirements of others.

CAN NARCISSISTIC PERSONALITY DISORDER (NPD) BE CURED?

Personality issues are incurable. The symptoms of the condition are treatable and can be diminished with the application of appropriate therapy and effort. However, there is always the possibility of reverting to previous thought and behavior patterns. Therapy is central to the management of NPD.

People with NPD learn the following through treatment:

Recognize the emotional foundations of their behavior and the reasons they've developed narcissistic behavior patterns.
Enhance interpersonal connections.
Abandon the pursuit of unattainable goals in favor of recognizing genuine talents and accomplishments.
Determine what drives their self-esteem.
Instead of seeking external affirmation, seeking personal validation.

Additionally, group, couple, and family therapy may be beneficial.
These are advantageous because they help individuals with NPD comprehend

how their behavior affects others. Unfortunately, there is a substantial obstacle to therapy. People with NPD are frequently unaware that their actions are problematic. This suggests they are oblivious of the negative consequences of their actions and may not care.

They are typically resistant to therapy and believe they do not require it. They may not benefit from therapy because they lack motivation to develop. There are no available medications to treat NPD. People with co-occurring maladies, such as depression and anxiety, may benefit from medications that treat their symptoms.

Couples

Throughout this book, we have examined how narcissists abuse those with whom they are in a relationship. A great deal of attention is paid to narcissistic abuse in romantic relationships because this is where the majority of people experience it. Given the significant emotional investment people make in their relationships, it is comprehensible that this type of abuse leaves the deepest wounds.

I will tell you things to watch out for not only in your partner but also in yourself. Frequently, we are overly preoccupied with ourselves and unable to observe the situation objectively. Consequently, the best course of action is to observe ourselves for subtle indicators of manipulation and our responses to it.

Patterns

Every narcissist adheres to a pattern. Beginning with love bombing, the relationship deteriorates into neglect and manipulation. If you're fortunate, you'll be able to recognize the signs of a love bomb and swiftly end the relationship. Completely disengaging from narcissists is the most effective method for coping with them. Any emotional investment you make will be exploited and used against you.

If your abuser removes their disguise as the relationship progresses, it will be difficult for you to escape the situation. At this juncture, you are fully emotionally invested, and severing ties will be difficult.

In narcissistic romantic relationships, punishment and minor rewards are typical. The narcissist will find methods to punish their partner if they don't get what they want or for no reason at all. They exert control through techniques such as withholding affection or "losing" or "breaking" something belonging to their companion.

All of this is merely a prelude to gaslighting, in which they turn their victim's accusations against them and cause them to doubt their reality. Occasionally, the attempt to exert control is overt, and the narcissist will threaten their partner. These threats need not be conveyed through clenched teeth. It can be a friendly reminder, for instance, that they will divulge humiliating information to a group that will undermine their victim.

Examples of overt threats include threatening to seize their partner's property or anything the couple shares, such as their residence or custody of their children. Invading their partner's privacy by monitoring their communications and messages is another tactic.

Typically, this is a diversionary tactic employed when their victim accuses them of infidelity or questions their whereabouts. In this manner, the narcissist deflects the accusations and accuses their victim of the exact same thing, i.e., they project their own flaws back onto their victims.

Relationship victims of narcissists are also cut off from their usual support system of friends and family. This can be gradual, making it difficult to detect over time because the victim either adapts to it or accepts the narcissist's explanation that the support network is to blame and threatening their relationship.

After a succession of arguments, narcissists will engage in love bombing and follow up with excessive displays of affection. The victim will be showered with gifts, unexpected surprises, and similar gestures. Because they have already invested so much time in the relationship, many victims will refuse to recognize these signals as indications of manipulation.

By performing such actions, the narcissist is simply luring their victim back, and as soon as the victim expresses affection, the narcissist becomes indifferent. The victim is left wondering what he did incorrectly as he returns to the same old routine. Other common narcissistic strategies for avoiding responsibility include diverting attention and constantly altering statements.

The narcissist will do nearly anything to avoid responsibility and will always attempt to misdirect the victim. For instance, a response to an accusation of infidelity might be that the home is dirty. This may seem nonsensical, but in a heated argument, the implication that the victim is to blame will not be overlooked.

Once the victim has expended all of her energy and is no longer able to fight back, the narcissist assumes complete control, as evidenced by the narcissist's control over their shared resources. At this stage, the victim has been fully absorbed into the narcissist's feeding group and is completely isolated from the outside world.

Examine Yourself

However, emotion has a way of confusing our minds. The most effective method of self-protection is to monitor yourself for any indicators of abuse. Thus, your attention will remain on yourself, and your judgment will not be influenced by the impressions of others.

Typically, the first symptom of abuse is when you find yourself repeatedly defending your abuser to your friends and family. I'm not referring to trivial infractions, such as forgetting to buy milk; rather, I'm referring to repeated concerns raised by your support network.

Since they perceive this as a personal assault on them and their decisions, many victims will defend their abusers to an extreme degree. This is precisely what the narcissist desires, as it functions to isolate others from their victim's life. Therefore, if you find yourself in this situation, keep in mind that there's a good possibility you're overlooking or ignoring something.

If you no longer care about your own goals and aspirations and instead associate them with sadness or regret, this is another clear indication of abuse.

This is a classic sign of abuse, as it indicates that the narcissist has effectively turned you against yourself and assimilated you into their emotional feeder network, or network of people who validate the narcissist.

If you continually place blame on yourself or suffer from anxiety or depression, look for signs of relationship abuse. The goal of the narcissist is to continually undermine you and erode your self-esteem. If you have observed this type of behavior in yourself, it may be a sign of maltreatment. Another subtle indicator is if you observe your companion acting differently around other people than they do with you.

Numerous victims will blame themselves for having offended the narcissist, which only exacerbates the anxiety cycle, which is followed by exhausting arguments and a love bomb.

And then you return to the same place of self-blame.

The most effective method to address all of this is to determine whether your partner is acting intentionally or unintentionally. Many narcissists are merely unaware of their behavior, and in some cases, counseling can be beneficial. If they genuinely want the relationship to succeed, even narcissists will strive to implement change and feel regret for their actions. Obviously, this situation is an exception.

Observe how they react and how they make you feel when you accuse them of something. There's a high chance that they're a narcissist if you feel awful and believe everything is your fault, or if they deflect and misdirect you. Try to bring this up as calmly as possible.

If they lack the motivation to transform, the relationship must be severed. This will be extremely painful, but always remember the first rule: Never injure yourself. The narcissist will accuse you of being self-centered, and if you have children, this will be exceedingly painful because the narcissist will do everything in their power to use them against you.

Do not commit the error of doing something for the sake of your offspring. If you choose to stay, they will only learn the incorrect method to deal with narcissism, setting them up to become either narcissists or victims themselves. Therefore, practice selfishness and self-compassion.

Relationship Based On Narcissism

Although narcissists have a reputation for being beasts incapable of forming healthy relationships, this is not how they begin. The narcissist hides behind a carefully crafted persona designed to attract and disarm unsuspecting targets, and can be found in a variety of relationships. Within these relationships, narcissists frequently follow the same pattern of employing the manipulation technique of love bombing, followed by demeaning and destroying the other person, and finally rejecting the relationship when something else comes along that the narcissist believes meets his or her needs better.

Relationship with a Narcissist that is Romantic

Despite their inability to genuinely adore anyone but themselves, narcissists frequently engage in romantic relationships. In the beginning, the narcissist may present himself as the ideal partner, leaving you in awe and with the impression that he is too wonderful to be true. He appears to be precisely what you've always desired, and with good reason. Narcissists have a propensity to reflect or mirror back exactly what they believe the other person desires to see in order to be perceived as superior or more desirable, thereby facilitating his access to the narcissistic supply he demands. You may encounter someone who is kind, considerate, and an excellent listener, but this phase is transient. This is the phase in which the narcissist attempts to learn everything about you in order to manipulate you later.

After gaining knowledge of you, he will employ it. If you have a hobby, he will adopt it and claim that he has always been a devoted follower. If you are looking for someone compassionate, he will fit the bill. If you are looking for a family man, he will boast about how frequently he sees his family and how close they are. If you desire to have children, he will describe how much he enjoys babysitting his nieces and nephews. Once the narcissist has attracted your attention, he commences his love bombing.

Simply stated, love bombing refers to the act of lavishing the other party with gifts, compliments, affection, and any other gestures of love. These will occur frequently and with an intensity you may have never experienced before meeting the narcissist; this intensity will essentially make you dependent on him. You associate him with the positive emotions you experienced during the love bombing phase. As a result, you will focus more time and energy on him than you would normally be comfortable with. You will feel as though you are in a fairy-tale whirlwind romance because he will advance the relationship as soon as possible. Sadly, the relationship is a fairy tale, but the conclusion is not what you might expect.

This honeymoon phase is short-lived, and as the relationship progresses, the narcissist's personality begins to erode. Initially, you may only catch a glimpse as he tests your tolerance to determine how much you will put up with before fleeing. This may involve ranting about someone else, snarling at you, or calling you derogatory names. After the fact, he will promise it will never happen again, although he will likely never apologize, and he hopes you will give him a second opportunity because you and he both love each other. Oftentimes, the narcissist's victim will attempt to excuse the outburst as a one-time occurrence, having been so shocked by the abrupt personality change. The narcissist's target will likely attempt to explain it away again in the future, perhaps with a slightly greater degree of intensity than before. Over time, the mask eventually erodes completely, and you are left staring at a stranger with the visage of the person you fell in love with. You may have become accustomed to the abuse and narcissistic behaviors, and you now find yourself in a relationship you never would have considered acceptable. This relationship may involve physical violence meant to intimidate you into submission, or it may consist solely of verbal or emotional abuse. In spite of this, the narcissist's victim frequently remains in the relationship, clinging to the belief that the person who initially captivated him or her is still present.

Even if you endure the narcissist's maltreatment, he will likely become bored with you and discard you over time. You may have lost your former allure, such as power, wealth, or self-assurance, and he becomes disinterested. Either he will have an affair to satisfy his narcissistic needs, or he will abandon you for someone else. The narcissist desires the honeymoon period, where everything is exciting and new, and as soon as the honeymoon period ends and the toy loses its luster, he is ready to move on to someone else.

Relationships with Narcissists

Similar to romantic relationships, narcissists initiate alliances with an intense honeymoon phase. Something about you has captured the attention of the narcissist, and she seeks to add you to her collection of supply sources. She will do everything possible to gain your favor and capture your attention. She may use her social standing to impress you by obtaining favors from people she believes may be of interest to you, such as persuading an acquaintance to make a reservation for you at a restaurant that is fully booked for the foreseeable future. She desires the acclaim that comes with being the savior who provides you with what you believed to be unattainable.

She, like a narcissistic romantic companion, will attempt to mirror you to make it appear as though you share more similarities with her than you actually do. She will even conduct research on your favored topics so that she can carry on conversations with you about them in order to gain your favor. As the friendship develops, it consumes you, drawing you away from other people you would typically communicate with, and you soon discover that she is your go-to friend for everything. You appreciate the aura of self-assurance and charisma that she has emanated, and you may feel as though the two of you are inseparable.

However, just as with the romantic companion, you will observe her mask slipping more and more over time. Every time you attempt to discuss a personal achievement or accomplishment, she will make it about herself. If you have just been accepted into a degree program for which you worked assiduously, she may congratulate you, but then make the conversation about herself. She may tell you how ecstatic she was when she was accepted into the program at the school that is more prestigious than the one you are attending, and how she feared she would not be able to live up to the school's standards, especially because she was caring for her mother during her battle with cancer, but she did it and was so proud. If you are getting married, she may announce her engagement or pregnancy during her toast to you, bringing attention to herself on your special day.

As your friendship grows, you will begin to recognize a pattern in which she feels compelled to continually outdo you. If you obtain a new position, she will seek a position with a higher status or higher pay. If you buy a new car because your old one was totaled in an accident, she will purchase a similar vehicle with even superior features and then laugh at the coincidence. She believes she must be the finest in her group, and her fragile ego cannot tolerate seeing others with superior possessions.

You will also observe that she is never available when you need her the most. Every time she has a problem, she expects you to abandon everything to attend to her needs or assist her, but she will not be there for you if you are ill, injured, or grieving. During your difficult time, she will mysteriously disappear, and when she eventually returns, she will make justifications for her absence that initially sound plausible, until a pattern emerges. You will be forced to choose between embracing the fact that she will never be there for you when you need her or ending the friendship altogether.

Collaboration with a Narcissist

You anticipate a certain level of courteous professionalism at work. You believe you should be able to work without fear of harassment or abuse, and the majority of companies would agree: There are entire divisions in many larger companies devoted to ensuring that you are treated fairly and without abuse. Despite the human resources department, narcissists are occasionally able to slip through the gaps. In accordance with their inherent desire to be the best and need to pursue power, narcissists are frequently found in positions of authority, such as supervisors or department managers.

Working under a narcissist can be extremely taxing, so if you have the misfortune of being employed by one, expect a certain degree of insensitivity.

Even if the employees' emotions are rational and justified, he disregards them because he lacks empathy and believes he is superior regardless. If you dare to ask for assistance, he will likely expect you to sort out the issue on your own and not cause a fuss. He may also attempt to shift responsibilities onto you in order to avoid them, and despite the extra effort you put in, he may deny you a raise or schedule you during a vacation you have been planning for months. To the narcissistic employer, you are little more than a company tool, comparable to one of the company's printers or computers, and you are expected to simply obey orders without complaint. Anything less than absolute obedience is offensive and intolerable.

Even if you complete more than your fair share of the work, the narcissistic boss will likely attempt to take credit for it, or may even choose to minimize the effort you did put in. After all, acknowledging that you had completed the task would detract from the success by diverting her attention. Even if you are great at your job, the narcissistic boss will not praise you. If your successes begin to make the narcissist feel threatened, he will often throw extra challenges at you to try to impede you, or order you to do something he knows you will fail in order to tarnish your reputation.

When working for a narcissistic employer, the narcissist will respond angrily whenever you attempt to point out a mistake or say something that is perceived as a challenge. True to his narcissistic nature, the supervisor cannot tolerate any criticism, and he will find a way to make the situation appear to be your fault, even if his reasoning is at best flawed.

Family Members Who Are Narcissistic

Narcissistic family relationships are among the most challenging to navigate. After all, you often hear that family members are the only people who will always have your back, regardless of the circumstances. Frequently, we feel obligated to maintain relationships with narcissistic family members, and because this obligation exists, the narcissist will exploit it. The narcissist views this blood connection as a shield that will allow her own narcissistic abuse to be tolerated much longer than anyone else would, particularly if the narcissist is a parent.

Typical narcissistic parents are ineffective and rarely produce healthy children. If a child reaches maturity without too many scars, it is not because of the parents but in spite of them. Typically, narcissistic parents are either extremely controlling of their child, viewing him or her as nothing more than an extension, or they are negligent and apathetic in the child. Occasionally, narcissistic parents are physically and emotionally abusive in general. Frequently, narcissistic mothers raise their children with the expectation that they will be ideal extensions of themselves as they navigate the world. Her offspring will be little more than extensions of her own body, and she will claim ownership of their home, property, and even successes.

As the child matures and naturally seeks independence, the narcissist's parenting methods intensify: Lacking the empathy required to recognize her children's needs, she begins enforcing control more and more, squelching any indications that her child is seeking independence. She will concentrate on the child's failures rather than nurturing and recognizing the successes, and she will use any means necessary, including cruelty or abuse, to bring the narcissist back into line.

When the narcissistic family member is not the child's parent, but rather a grandparent, aunt, uncle, or other relative, they frequently attempt to use the young child as a source of narcissistic supply. Following the typical love-bombing phase, they frequently lavish young children with gifts while neglecting older children who are able to form their own opinions. As the child ages, however, and begins to see the world for what it is and express concerns or disagreements, he or she is frequently abandoned, particularly if the family has a younger child. This can be extremely detrimental to young children, who go from being lavished with love and attention to being abruptly rejected and shunned.

However, when the child becomes an adult, he or she is expected to pander to the narcissist's every whim in the name of the family, even though nothing will ever be sufficient. If not stopped, this cycle is likely to repeat through generations and can be extremely detrimental to the minds of young children.

Co-Parenting with an Ex-Partner Who Is Narcissistic

Co-parenting is never simple, but co-parenting with narcissists is a completely different ballgame. When relationships fail without children, the dissolution is typically swift and permanent, whereas when children are involved, the relationship can never be completely severed. As a result, even if you divorce or abandon a narcissist, you may be compelled to maintain some level of contact with your ex-spouse if you share children with him or her.

If there is a court order mandating co-parenting, you will be required to offer your child to the narcissist even if you would prefer not to. Because of this, the narcissist uses the children to manipulate and harm you frequently. He will not hesitate to throw the children under the proverbial bus in order to hurt you the same way you wounded him when you initiated the separation. He may refuse to take the children because you had plans during his parenting time and it is too late to find a sitter, or he may choose to take parenting time or phone calls during disruptive periods. Ultimately, he cares only about causing you pain in any way imaginable.

Typically, narcissists want to appear as desirable and commendable as possible, but they want to do so with minimal effort. Even if he takes the children for his parenting time because he knows you cannot stand to be separated from them, he may not provide for their needs, such as maintaining their hygiene or preparing nutritious meals. He may also take the children in order to hand them over to his relatives, particularly if you dislike certain members of his family, because it saves him the trouble and he is uninterested in his children.

You must also be prepared for the narcissist to perform mind games with his children. During an argument, he may cease giving them any attention or affection, and he will always place the blame on you to make you appear worse in the eyes of your children. He will claim that you told him he could not do something or made him so furious that he could not take the children to the amusement park as promised. This strategy, known as parental alienation, is intended to harm you by driving a wedge between you and your offspring.

Given the above, it is evident that narcissists are rarely effective co-parents. They prioritize themselves above all else and will not act in the best interests of their offspring simply because that is what parents do. Without the ability to empathize with his children, he will always act selfishly and will never be an effective parent.

The easiest way to deal with a narcissist in a co-parenting relationship is to minimize contact and document everything. Do not speak negatively about the other parent of your child, and allow the child to make decisions regarding the narcissistic parent without your influence. The most important thing to consider when co-parenting with a narcissist is to provide your child with support during this challenging time.

The Narcissist's True Self Is The False Self.

Generally, narcissists are prone to substance abuse, such as drug abuse and excessive alcohol consumption. In addition, they frequently experience depression and are prone to relationship difficulties. In addition, they experience difficulties at work or school. Worse still, they entertain suicidal ideas and display suicidal tendencies.

According to a study published in PLoS One, males with narcissistic personality disorder have very high levels of cortisol, a specific stress hormone, in their blood, and this is prevalent even when they are experiencing low levels of stress. Even in such circumstances, they have high tension levels. However, the elevated level of this hormone in narcissistic men is associated with a very high risk of cardiovascular disease.

Despite the fact that a person with this disorder may appear innocuous, as if the disorder does not have many negative effects, it is a mental health issue that can lead to a number of other complications if it is not properly addressed and treated. The narcissistic personality disorder has repercussions that can have a negative impact on the individual's mental and physical health, as well as his social life.

Typically, narcissists may view themselves as too superior to pursue treatment or assistance. It is therefore of the utmost importance to realize that this disorder significantly impacts the lives of your loved ones. Those who are afflicted with this mental health condition will benefit greatly from a support system from their loved ones who appreciate and support their decision to seek appropriate treatment and therapy. Next, we will examine some negative consequences of narcissistic personality disorder.

Workplace Partnerships

It is not at all surprising to find narcissists in positions of authority in the workplace, as they typically present themselves as dominant individuals. You will frequently observe them sounding their trumpets. They frequently boast about their accomplishments, so when they attain positions of authority, they are likely to alienate their colleagues and subordinates.

Typically, narcissist leaders will exhibit selfish and exploitative leadership styles, but their character defects will eventually manifest and be revealed to everyone. Their arrogant attitudes cause them to devalue others and even disregard corporate regulations. When they are in need of something or a favor from a coworker, they exhibit a charming side; however, they are always insensitive to the emotions and plights of others and dismissive of any task they deem beneath them.

Additionally, they tend to be envious of those they perceive as more accomplished than themselves. Typically, when people first begin working, they establish early milestones with early accomplishments, but later in their careers, they begin to regress.

Community And Social Relations

In the context of their immediate social and community environment, narcissists are typically not far from interpersonal conflicts, as they significantly contribute to their occurrence. The majority of the time, they gravitate toward those they believe will portray them favorably, which may contribute significantly to social ascending.

How Might Your Crisis Develop?

Numerous studies have examined the impact of NPD on intimate partner relationships. As you may already have surmised, this disorder has a negative impact on intimate relationships. At the outset of this type of relationship, narcissists typically appear charming, confident, and exciting because they tend to attract people who are interested in drama and are caretakers in the hope that they will be able to correct the narcissist's character flaws.

When the individual with this disorder is a wealthy, attractive, or talented man, he typically finds ways to persuade his partner that he is attempting to start a new relationship with a clean slate, despite the failure of his previous relationship. However, over time he progressively loses interest and commitment to the point where he is unable to make an emotional investment in the relationship.

Various negative attitudes, including arrogance, a sense of entitlement, resentment, sensitivity to criticism, and the need for attention, begin to emerge. All of these indicators point to imminent turmoil in the narcissist's relationships. They are always on the lookout for a better companion, and as a result, they are always prone to promiscuity.

Narcissists find admiration from others to be very attractive and also addictive; therefore, when their partners discover their dysfunctional personality, problems arise, and they receive fewer compliments from their partners.

For a person with NPD, forming interpersonal relationships is always very simple. Initially, they find it simple to enjoy these new relationships, but later, their narcissistic traits interfere with the newly formed relationship. People with this disorder are preoccupied with themselves and have difficulty forming relationships with others.

When narcissists are the ones who have caused relationship problems, they find it extremely simple to create excuses for themselves. Later, they begin to speculate about a prosperous future. In most cases, they exhibit characteristics of self-entitled behavior and assign blame for everything that has gone wrong as quickly as possible, particularly when things do not go according to plan. They are also eager to accept credit when things go well.

Control is also extremely essential to narcissists because they cannot tolerate the idea of losing their facade. Those who are in a relationship with narcissists only realize how difficult it is to be in a relationship with them once they are already in one. This fact makes the relationship with a narcissist tragic and complicated.

When narcissists perceive a potential threat to their egos or a sense of rejection, their initial response will be wrath and aggression. At such times, narcissists begin to display narcissistic fury, a concept associated with the NPD that is extremely disturbing.

However, narcissistic rage is described as an outburst of explosive, self-gratifying anger that may be displayed at a rapid tempo and is always a reaction to any perceived insult. When a narcissist is in this state of fury, all other humans are rendered insignificant and subhuman. Others may view this anger as an inappropriate or exaggerated response. Narcissists frequently neglect that other people have been valuable or kind to them in the past, or that other people also have the right to exist. Despite the fact that this is a delusional disorder, those with it are able to rewrite the past to make their transgressions appear acceptable. To conform to their delusions, they may embellish or even fabricate information.

Chronic bitterness is another aspect of wrath associated with the narcissist in terms of interpersonal relationships. It is not uncommon for narcissists to harbor grievances against those they perceive to have wronged them, and they devote a significant portion of their time to devising schemes to rectify even the most trivial of perceived wrongs. However, they may initiate their pursuit for vengeance out of narcissistic rage.

Even if a person was raised by a narcissistic parent, it does not predispose them to develop the disorder, according to research.

However, it is extremely challenging for narcissistic parents to model stable relationships. When a parent suffers from this disorder, he or she will struggle to form attachments to his or her child or children. Parenting will always be hindered by the parent's superior intelligence, arrogance, and selfishness.

Because personality disorders are always characterized by problematic interpersonal relationships, parents with personality disorders always have problematic parenting tendencies. According to research, personality disorders are associated with high parental rejection and possessiveness. Poor communication, low parental affection, inconsistent discipline, little time spent with the child, a lack of positive reinforcement, and inadequate parental supervision have also been linked to parents with personality disorders (Sybil, 2012). In contrast to the literature on intimate relationships, there is a dearth of research on narcissistic parenting (Sybil, 2012). Consequently, there is a need for further study in this area.

Therapeutic Partnerships

The majority of individuals with NPD find it extremely difficult to seek treatment from mental health professionals. In the majority of cases, patients are more likely to seek medical care for anxiety, depression, or other mental health issues related to their inability to maintain interpersonal relationships with their family, colleagues, coworkers, or intimate partners. Patients with this disorder prefer to avoid therapeutic relationships, which is exacerbated by the fact that they always speak to others in a demeaning or devaluing manner, despite the fact that they can also appear charming and beguiling.

When interacting with a narcissist, it is crucial to maintain distinct boundaries; therefore, a thorough understanding of the disorder's symptoms is necessary to successfully work with/on patients. When they finally submit themselves to therapy, they find it much simpler to minimize their symptoms, despite harboring deep-seated fears.

In order to facilitate successful therapeutic relationships with the narcissist, it is preferable to reassure the patient that he or she is completely understood. Therapists must have empathy for narcissists in order to cope with the inherent grandiosity of these patients. Therapists must ensure that they recognize the requirements of narcissistic patients.

The Self-Centered Parent

You may have pondered on multiple occasions whether a narcissistic parent affects the child's upbringing. While this does not necessarily indicate that a child raised by a narcissistic parent will become a narcissist, it does speak volumes about the parental skills of the narcissistic parent. Growing up with such parents is detrimental for both the child and the co-parent.

It is crucial to observe that boastfulness alone does not qualify someone as a narcissist. People typically misidentify as narcissists those who are egotistical, arrogant, or overly focused on themselves. Despite the fact that these characteristics are irritating and uncool, narcissism is much more profound in reality. It is a destructive disorder with devastating consequences for those in a relationship with the narcissist. Although many individuals believe that the disorder cannot be treated, the reality is that, despite its difficulty, it is treatable. Let us examine the actual effects of the disorder when it affects a caregiver. The effects of narcissistic parenting on children include the following:

There will be little or no recognition of the child's reality or emotions.

The parent will regard the child as an accessory as opposed to a person.

The child will not perceive being heard or seen.

The child will be valued solely for the things he or she does, particularly for the parents, and not for who he or she is as an individual.

The child will develop debilitating self-doubt because he or she has never learned to trust or recognize his or her own emotions.

The child will incorrectly believe that his or her appearance is more important than how he or she feels.

The child will fear being genuine, and will believe that his or her image is more essential than being genuine.

The child will be taught to keep secrets in order to protect his or her parents and the family, regardless of the repercussions of doing so.

Typically, the child will perceive that he or she is being used and manipulated.

The parents will not instruct the child on how to develop an independent sense of self.

The child will have difficulty placing his or her trust in others.

The child will experience a great deal of emotional desolation and will believe that he or she is not nurtured.

Instead of the parent being there for the child, the child will be there for the parent at all times.

The child will experience considerable frustration as he or she seeks affection, attention, and approval in vain.

The child will have emotionally stunted development.

Instead of feeling accepted and adored, the child will experience constant criticism and evaluation.

The child will grow up with the belief that he or she is inadequate.

When it comes to learning how to form emotional connections, the child will have no role model.

The child will be prone to taking care of others at the expense of his or her own needs; consequently, he or she will lack appropriate self-care skills and will be more likely to be codependent.

The youngster will learn to pursue external validation rather than internal validation.

- Individualization from the parent will be difficult for the child, which is crucial as the child matures.

- The infant will not be able to set or respect appropriate relationship boundaries.

- Instead of teaching the child to aspire to surpass the parent, he or she will be instructed to work diligently to earn the parent's admiration.

- The parent may become envious of the child if the child is performing better than the parent.

The child will be reluctant to receive credit, even if it is credit he or she deserves.

As a result of his narcissistic parent's incessant shaming and humiliation, the child will eventually develop a low sense of self-worth.

Eventually, as an adult, the child will experience some measure of post-traumatic stress disorder, depression, or even anxiety.

Since he did not receive any form of parental affection while he was growing up, he will feel unlovable and contemptible. If his parents are unable to adore him, who will?

The infant may become either a self-saboteur or a high achiever, or possibly both. When the child reaches adulthood, he or she will have to undergo trauma recovery and may even have to re-parent themselves.

When a child is raised by a narcissistic parent, he or she will endure severe psychological and emotional maltreatment, which will have debilitating and long-lasting consequences. Professionals frequently fail to recognize narcissism because narcissists are adept at presenting themselves in an appealing manner by painting only the image of themselves that they want others to see. While the children struggle with suffocation, loneliness, and suffering behind closed doors, the narcissist portrays a different image to the public.

Narcissists never accept responsibility for their errors, instead blaming others, particularly children. The result is that the child begins to believe that he or she is responsible for every error and act of misbehavior, whether or not he or she is at fault. Typically, mental health professionals and therapists must deal with such symptoms. Even though the lifestyles and stories vary, the emotive banner remains constant.

A co-parent with the narcissist or a member of the extended family who is attempting to eliminate the effects of narcissistic parenting will need to exert double the effort to maintain their responsibility. The best method to accomplish this is to be an empathic parent, the opposite of narcissism.

Professionals working on cases involving narcissistic parents will need to acquire knowledge of the disorder. They should avoid downplaying the severity of the disorder. In addition, these professionals should ensure that the children are present in therapy in order to learn how to be emotionally assertive, a skill they will apply to their emotionally distant parents. Putting children first is the most essential action to take.

Due to the fact that NPD is a spectrum disorder, it is essential to approach it as a continuum. Everyone exhibits narcissistic traits that have the potential to manifest as a full-fledged personality disorder. The greater a person's level of narcissism, the more harm he or she is capable of causing to other individuals.

Cultivate Reciprocal Relationships
Ask for help

You are not alone, and many people have experienced or are experiencing what you are going through. Don't be afraid to ask for help and find a support system to offer you what you need to stay balanced, secure, and self-confident in your choices and journey forward.

It has never been your fault that the person you are in a relationship with doesn't understand their disorder or issue, and even if you were capable of enabling it for a long period of time, you are certainly capable of healing from it and learning how not to repeat the same patterns over and over again.

Help is always available and all around you. If you cannot get to a public support group, or feel comfortable talking to friends and family about it, go online and look for more resources. Find an anonymous group to join if you want to protect your identity. Ask other people what it was like for them and how their recovery process is going. You will learn so much by simply reaching out for help and letting it clear your fears that you are somehow at fault for your experience.

All it takes is awareness and courage, as you let go of the narcissistic relationship. Empowering yourself to enjoy your life more through a balanced partnership is what any person deserves, and you are on the right track to getting there. Heal the patterns so that they are broken and cannot be repeated by offering yourself kindness, staying personal with your journey, process your emotions regularly, take the high road, know the red flags of the narcissist, and seek help whenever you feel like you need support.

You are on your way to becoming the confident, happy, and balanced person you always knew you are and could be. Learning to survive the narcissistic relationship may seem hard at first, but you have all of the tools that you need to accept your story and begin the healing journey.

It is wrong to be in a one-sided relationship with someone who cares only about himself. Such a relationship never ends well, and it is better to see a professional who will help you deal with this kind of situation. In most cases, you are powerless in dealing with such people because they are usually over-possessive. They emotionally trap you into staying in an unhealthy relationship because they feel you belong to them. And they always find a way to blame you for whatever is wrong in the relationship. They are perfect at shifting the blames to the weaker person in the relationship. They play with your emotions and use them against you. That is why, in most cases, you feel like you are in prison. You will be emotionally blackmailed into not seeing walking away as an option.

A mental health professional, however, will help you deal with the relationship right. Sometimes, walking away might not be the solution; you can go through a "pro-dependence oriented" treatment that will help you remain in the relationship but in a much healthier way. The concept of the pro-dependence is to consider the advantage of living with people who challenge us, and channeling our focus on how we benefit from them, rather than considering the vices and dreading what suffering might result in enduring such relationship. We can benefit a whole lot from their strengths. Also, they can gain from us. In reality, you can turn the relationship into a give-and-take thing where both of you end up benefiting from each other.

Probably the best way to cope with the aftermath of breaking it off with a narcissist is finding yourself a decent support group. There are lots of internet-based and real-life groups that you can find in order to discover the stories of others who have been through experiences similar to yours.

Finding individuals who have had run-ins with narcissists in their lives can make it easier to understand that you were never the problem and that these people actually exist in the world. The sooner you get to grasp the reality that narcissists are at fault for their own failed relationships, the sooner you can forgive yourself for allowing the abuse to occur.

In the same light, you might also want to find someone who can shed insight on your unique feelings. Therapists who are well-versed with narcissistic abuse can help you understand your emotions and uncover the truths behind the behaviours of your narcissistic abuser. These people can also provide you valuable coping skills and activities that can make the healing process faster and much more satisfying.

No contact

For the first few days or weeks after you've finally cut the ties, you might feel the nagging urge to come crawling back and say you're sorry. In typical victim fashion, you might feel like you've done something immensely wrong, leading you to think that you need to offer an apology for acting the way you did.

At this point, you need to remind yourself why you left in the first place. Remind yourself of the abuse and put things into perspective. Recall the pain, the abandonment, the criticism, and the devaluation and realize that these were all real experiences that weren't pleasant for you at all.

Avoid blaming yourself and avoid contact with your abuser at all costs. Give yourself the time to heal and to see things through clear, untainted glasses instead of the blinds that the narc placed over your eyes. If you must, consider taking a break from social media and keeping your phone away from you for the time being. Preoccupy yourself with a hobby and keep your mind busy so you don't end up thinking about your narcissistic abuser.

Is it always right to leave a narcissist?

Rejecting a narcissist, whether in reality or in their perception, is likely to make them feel incredibly hurt or angry- as it causes a deep narcissistic injury. A jilted lover may feel a great deal of pain when the source of their affection no longer wants them. So, too, a narcissist feels deeply aggrieved when a source of narcissistic supply- or anyone else for that matter- decides that they are not "good enough."

Extreme narcissists – ever hypervigilant- may feel rejected for reasons that more average people would not. Being too busy or not having a good enough reason to deny their request for your company or collaboration can easily be taken to heart and result in an unexpectedly intense response. It's best to give them a legitimate reason that is beyond your control than to show that you're choosing to reject them. Being too busy to meet or see them is best if your reason is irrefutable, like having to work late to meet a specific deadline, attend an important wedding, or are booked onto a vacation or trip elsewhere.

Narcissists do not like losing

They really don't. When you say that your relationship is finished, you mean it but the narcissist you are talking to sees that as you throwing down a gauntlet, an invitation to kick into high narcissistic mode and see it as a real challenge and that leads you to:

Narcissists Pursue Victory

He or she won't be chasing after you although that's what it will look like. No, instead they are looking to put things back to how they should be, with them in full control and you bowing down and taking the abuse, while smothering them in adoration and praise. Believe me when I say this, if you give in and do go back, there will be some form of punishment for the abandonment. He or she does want you back but only on their terms and with the same, if not a higher, degree of selfishness and narcissistic behaviour that was there when you left – why you left.

Narcissists want to keep a constant check on you

Because he or she still loves you? Not likely. Let's face it; they probably never really loved you in the true sense. All he or she wants to do is make sure that you are suffering, that you are not happy and never will be without them in your life. To a narcissist, it is the knowledge that you are truly miserable and suffering without him or her is as satisfying as getting you to go back to them.

At the end of the day, if he or she cannot keep your attention on him or her throughout the relationship then they will want to know that you are constantly thinking of them and really struggling after you are apart. At some point, he or she will offer to end the suffering by accepting your apology and taking you back. Big mistake – once you are back under their control the abuse will begin again and it will never stop. The most satisfying thing to a narcissist is having you swaying between being with him or her and leaving – that gives the control over you, the ultimate prize for a narcissist.

How to Leave

As long as you are still under the spell of a narcissist, you will be unable to move ahead successfully. This is why it is vital that you leave the person before you can make headway in everything that you do.

However, since you have been in the relationship for a long time, and maybe you two have kids together, you will find it hard to leave the partner.

However, with the right tips, you can leave the person successfully.

Here are the various tips to help you get away from an abusive relationship safely.

Don't Give Them the Last Chance

When you leave an abusive narcissist, they will try to seduce you so that you come back to them and then they will dump you. The main aim of a narcissist is to make sure you are the one to blame in everything.

They want everything to be on their terms, and when it isn't, they find a way to turn the tables around. If the narcissist isn't ready to leave yet, they will turn on the works and plead with you, begging you and telling you how sorry they are.

For you to leave, try and avoid giving them a chance to have the power over you again. They will turn on the begging and then they will plead with you so much, saying how sorry they are and beg you to come back.

Don't Let Them Know You Are Leaving

You don't need to tell the narcissist that you are leaving the relationship. This is because it might make them ready to start love bombing you to trap you in the relationship. They can even threaten to kill themselves just to make you stay on, and they trap you.

Have Some Spare Cash

When you think of leaving, you need to make sure you have some spare cash to get you started with the new life. Start saving some money early in advance so that when the time comes you leave, you don't have to come back to the person because of the support that they give you.

If your partner is an abuser, then you need to do everything in secret so that the person doesn't cut you off entirely.

Report the Abuse

You might not be in the right position to take the situation to the police, but it is vital that you report the abuse. When you go in, make sure you tell what has been happening to you, and you even show the injuries in case you have any that are visible.

When you record a statement, you will have something that you can report when you decide to make a case later on in the future.

Log Out of All Devices

If you stay logged into devices that you shared with your partners, you need to make sure that you change the passwords to devices so that the partner doesn't track you. Make a reset of all the credentials and create new ones.

So, make a list of everything that you have ever signed into, used your credit card on and any autofill, then delete them all.

After logging out of the devices, the next thing is to make sure you aren't being tracked. If possible, dispose of off the phone then get a new one that you can use.

Don't Be Swayed By the Flattery

A narcissist will try and use flattery or any other approach to prevent you from leaving. The goal is to create an environment where you feel that you don't have a choice but to leave.

The narcissist will try to be more than what you ever wanted, and they will do this in various ways, including buying your gifts and giving you the attention you always desired.

Reconnect With Family and Friends

An abusive narcissist will want to cut you away from the family and take up their attention. You might not have been with some of the people that were previously close to you, and you might have neglected them. But the most important thing is for you to reconnect with them so that they assist you in healing.

However, you need to stop feeling shy and embarrassed when they see you. If you have to say sorry, then swallow your pride and apologize.

When you reconnect with them, you will realize how much the people had planned to help you with no success. They might have tried to help, but they didn't know what to do or how to start.

Clean the Decks

This is the right time to identify anyone toxic to your cause and then let them go. You will make a decision, but not everyone will be as understanding as you expect them to be. They will point fingers at you and pretend they are the best in the world.

You need to take this as an opportunity to cut out some people from your life, especially those that are toxic to your goals.

How to deal with a complicated relationship when children are involved

Dealing with someone who is narcissistic can be tedious, draining, and at times, downright painful, particularly if you are gaining nothing from it. It is even worse when there are children involved. You can begin by seeing if there are any areas that you can change your perspective on. Although you may not like the idea of changing yourself, particularly when the one with narcissism should change, it might be a good place to start.

There are also those who already have children, and do not want to deny them the chance of being raised by both parents. Yet others cite financial reasons; he may be a narcissist, but he's paying the bills.

Choosing to stay is a valid choice. You can take control of the relationship and ensure that you do not suffer in the process.

Set boundaries

This is the first step in making sure that your partner does not walk all over you. Make a list of the things that you will not tolerate. This could include name-calling, criticism, threats, yelling, lying, and making demands, and so on. It is important to write them down as proof.

Disrespecting the boundaries should have consequences. If you told your man that the moment he starts shouting, you'll walk away and sleep in the guest bedroom; do just that. He will try to manipulate you to soften your resolve. If you do so, he'll know that he can get away with it. He'll keep pushing the boundaries, and within no time you'll be right back where you started.

Did he change when you decided to set boundaries? You may want to control the way he speaks to you, then he decides not to speak to you at all. He gives you the silent treatment. This shows that he does not appreciate the boundaries. Don't worry. He doesn't need to. He only needs to appreciate that they're important for the sake of your relationship.

Bring up such conversations when he's in a good mood. He's more likely to listen then.

Listen

People hardly ever listen to narcissists. As soon as they start speaking; people around them are thinking, 'oh, here we go again with the grand talk.' They mentally switch off. And you can hardly blame them. Self-exalting talk is exhausting you know.

Listen to him for a change. He may be praising himself or playing victim yet again, but listen to him anyway. He'll see that you're interested in his welfare, and this will encourage them to treat you better.

Stay Calm

How you behave in times of conflict goes a long way in determining the nature of your relationship with a narcissist. He will try to provoke you into a reaction so that he can convince himself that he has control over your emotions. Your ability to stay calm robs him of that power.

If things seem to be getting out of hand, you can seek help together. Hearing the effect of his behaviour from a neutral party might provoke him to do some soul searching and eventually take steps towards changing.

Narcissist Mothers

Before you encounter a narcissist in a relationship, it's likely that you've encountered similar behavior in your family. A narcissistic mother or parent strikes the nearest to home. Given that we enter the world as defenseless infants, it is extremely perplexing and uneasy. Our parents are expected to protect and care for us. And as infants, we trust and rely on them instinctively. While the majority of parents do the best they can, some deliberately do the worst they can.

What is the definition of a narcissistic mother?

I, myself, and I am responsible. No one else should ever endeavor to steal the spotlight.

In essence, this is what a narcissistic mother is all about.

Self-love is necessary so that we can appreciate and care for ourselves and show others how they should treat us, but the narcissistic mother is all about herself. She has a strong sense of entitlement and is extremely self-absorbed. She is exempt from the rule that applies to everyone else.

She lacks empathy for everyone other than herself, whether she is a grandiose narcissist who must be the loudest or the brightest or a fragile person who must compete over who has endured the most. Occasionally, there is both a race to the bottom and a race to the summit.

She may even enjoy seeing her own offspring suffer as she engages in manipulative behavior.

When we refer to narcissistic personality disorder (NPD) in psychology and psychiatry, what we really mean by "personality disorder" is that this affects their relationships, employment, and overall well-being. Thus the qualification "personality." And a person with NPD cannot and will not transform.

The Six Facial Expressions of Maternal Narcissism

The affliction of narcissistic parenting causes significant emotional damage to children. Children raised by narcissistic parents grow up in denial, believing it is their responsibility that they are not good enough if they are not acknowledged. If exceptional enough, that parent would have loved them.

Although this is a cognitive distortion of the self, the abundance of internal signals that narcissistic parents' adult children receive from infancy has a worrisome effect. "Will I ever be good enough?" "Am I lovable?" "Am I simply appreciated for what I do and how I look?" "Can I trust my own feelings?" Does this sound familiar?

The term "narcissism" is becoming more common, but it is primarily used to disparage others. It is not humorous, is sometimes misunderstood, and is typically used to describe someone who is haughty or arrogant. In reality, genuine narcissism is a dreadful disease that harms children.

Narcissists are truly self-centered and incapable of authentic empathy. Their capacity to offer their offspring unconditional love is limited. The unsettling outcomes are cause for concern.

Identifying parental narcissism is not about aiding another victim group. The purpose is not to harbor hatred, blame, resentment, or rage against that parent. It is about compassion, knowledge, and comprehension in order for healing to occur.

Children and parents require some points of connection in order to recover and develop a deeper template. Being able to detect internal childhood signals is crucial for innumerable individuals. Frequently, a parent with narcissistic tendencies is not a full-blown narcissist. The influence of knowledge may aid in repairing past damage.

True, it is doubtful that a full-blown narcissist will change, but an adult child may engage in personal rehabilitation efforts.

The six aspects of mother narcissism are characterized as follows: the flamboyant-extrovert, the achievement-oriented, the psychosomatic, the addicted, the covertly nasty, and the emotionally needy. Typically, a parent possesses a combination of these characteristics.

The Flamboyant Extrovert: This is the mother who inspires blockbusters. She is a public performer who is admired by the audiences but feared by her housemates and children. She is the mother of the entertainment industry and is a performance fanatic. She is noticeable, ostentatious, vivacious, and "out there." Others adore her, but you despise the mask she constructs for the world. You realize that you are irrelevant to her and her program, except for how you portray her to the outside world.

The Achievement-Focused: For the achievement-oriented mother, your life's accomplishments are crucial. What you do determines your success, not who you are. This article focuses on grades, top universities, and necessary degrees. But... if you do not do what she believes you should, she is deeply humiliated and may resort to violence.

The Psychosomatic: A psychosomatic mother uses illness and aches and pains to manipulate others, get her way, and draw attention to herself. She has little regard for those around her. To attract the attention of this type of mother, it is necessary to care for her. This type of mother uses illness as a means of avoiding her own emotions or dealing with problems. You cannot be more ill than she.

A parent with a substance abuse problem will always appear egotistical, as the addiction will speak loudly than anything else. Sometimes, when an addict sobers up, the narcissism subsides, but this is not always the case. The bottle or prescribed medication will always take precedence over the child.

The covertly Cruel: The covertly cruel mother hides the fact that she abuses her children from others. She will have a public persona and a private personality that are distinctly separate. These mothers may be kind and compassionate in public, but they are severe and cruel at home. The unexpected, contradictory signals are driving the child insane.

While all narcissistic mothers are emotionally needy, this mother displays this trait more overtly than the others. This is the mother for whom the child must provide emotional support, which is disadvantageous for the child. The child's feelings are ignored, and he or she is unlikely to receive the same care that he or she is expected to provide for the parent.

Identifying a Narcissist

Four Strategies for Handling Narcissists in the Workplace

If a parent possessed any of the aforementioned characteristics, it is crucial to remember that they were not born with them. As children, they surely faced insurmountable obstacles in acquiring affection and compassion. This does not alleviate your suffering. We will never tolerate juvenile abuse. However, this information facilitates a deeper comprehension.

If your mirror is vacant and you did not receive adequate care as a child, as an adult you must remember that healing is the solution. It is predominantly internal labor that must be completed. The five-step procedure of rehabilitation is described in Will I Ever Be Good Enough? Restoring the Health of Narcissistic Mothers' Daughters. Once we comprehend, we can establish an internal mother who is always there when you need her, unlike a narcissistic mother who is always there for herself.

The Offspring of Narcissistic Mothers

How narcissistic women destroy and influence their offspring.

Every offspring of a narcissist suffers. The autonomy, self-worth, and prospective relationships with women of sons of narcissistic mothers are compromised.

Narcissists lack empathy and parental nurturing skills. They do not view them as individuals, but rather as extensions of themselves. The emotions and needs of their children are disregarded and mocked, while their own are prioritized.

Narcissists have a sense of entitlement and demand their own way. Compliance exacted by means of control, manipulation, guilt, and humiliation. It's "their way or the highway," and if you don't comply, they will penalize you with hostility, indifference, or withholding. Insecurity fuels their insatiable, irrational desire for esteem and admiration.

They are readily offended, resulting in contempt and rage. Because they lack boundaries, they project—they humiliate and blame others for their inability to manage their own emotional anguish.

Sons' relationships with narcissistic mothers are dynamic.

The degree and type of narcissism varies with each individual's personality and values. Some narcissistic mothers are indifferent to their offspring, while others are overly involved. Some behave in an antagonistic manner, whereas others appear compassionate or alluring. The following are common patterns, but your experience may differ.

Neglect

When overwhelmed by motherhood, narcissistic mothers neglect their children, then humiliate and condemn them, sometimes for being overly dependent or infantile. They are in need and cannot endure their child's needs. They may encourage their young son to "be a man," or they may favor one child while neglecting or disparaging another.

Enmeshment

Instead of neglect, other narcissistic mothers are entangled with their children. They use their offspring as a source of narcissism. Although a mother may appear independent, she may be emotionally dependent and nurture her son's mutual dependence through possessive and authoritarian behavior. She may rely on her son to provide emotional support, to listen to her, to be her companion, and to take care of her physical requirements and responsibilities. She may rely on him to make decisions and manage her affairs and finances when he is an adult.

She uses and exploits her child primarily to receive attention and adoration, and to satisfy her own desires and needs. She makes him feel loved, valued, and cherished, which increases his reliance. However, only at her discretion. Therefore, her excessive involvement with her child may conceal her toxic parenting. His aspirations for autonomy generally come with a hefty price tag. Through her manipulation using wrath, humiliation, remorse, self-pity, and/or martyrdom, he learns and feels compelled to prioritize her demands and needs.

Perfectionism and Criticism

Many narcissistic mothers view their young sons as ideals. They enhance his self-assurance and sense of significance. As he matures and challenges her authority, she criticizes his burgeoning individuality and attempts to mold him. She may boast about her son to her acquaintances in order to boost her ego, but she is critical at home. In response, he may either rebel and incur her wrath or attempt to appease her in order to be accepted.

His fall from grace may be perplexing and troubling. It is frustrating when another child is delivered. He loses his uniqueness, which may intensify sibling rivalry.

It is worse for a son if his father is absent, violent, mentally ill, or addicted to drugs. Then, to endure, the son may seek solace in substance abuse or strengthen his bond with his mother.

Seduction and "Oedipal" complications

In instances in which the mother is seductive and sexualizes her relationship with her son, the situation can be more detrimental. Even in the absence of molestation, emotional incest can occur when mothers engage in inappropriate language, appearance, and behavior with their sons. She is captivating and alluring to a young man. This overstimulates his probable (but typically unconscious) maternal affinity. Ideally, a child will grow closer to his father and view him as a masculine role model. When the father is absent or when a divorced mother demeans and alienates her ex-husband, this risk is increased.

Unresolved, some boys may incorrectly presume that their mother loves them more than her spouse. Instead of conceding defeat, he is cocky and victorious over his father. This dynamic harms the adult intimate relationships of the offspring. Since he views his father, who should be a positive role model, failing, it may also impair his masculine self-concept.

The nurturing relationship between a father and his son facilitates their bonding and the son's resolution of inner conflicts.

In the same way that daughters of narcissistic mothers experience their mother's envy and competition, a narcissistic mother may be envious of her son's companions and in competition with his wife.

No one will be acceptable because no one will meet her inflated self-perception and expectations. She must remain his number one priority. She may try to dominate and undermine his personal relationships, disparage or demean his spouse, or do so covertly through innuendo and manipulation.

Trying to avoid hurting and angering his mother and fiancé (who may also be a narcissist or otherwise psychologically unstable) (who may also be a narcissist or otherwise psychologically unstable), her child may feel hopelessly guilty and caught in the middle. He is miserable, uncertain of permissible limits, and unable to set them.

The Effects of Narcissistic Mothers on Their Sons

Similarly to sons of narcissistic fathers, sons of narcissistic mothers do not feel adored for who they are, but rather for what they can do to earn their parents' approval. Due to the importance of appearance, parents must ensure that their children's appearance and behavior reflect favorably on them.

If presented at all, love is contingent. It is not based on understanding, appreciating, and embracing their son's unique, genuine self. The son's worth is determined by the degree to which he elevates his parents' ideals and vanity. This may include exerting pressure on him to enter the parent's preferred profession and attain success or the lifestyle his parents desire.

Codependency

Whether or not boys achieve success in the world, they run the danger of becoming insecure and dependent. Their uniqueness has never been acknowledged. Verbal abuse and a lack of empathy for their true self have eroded their sense of self-worth and self-esteem. They learned to appease their mother by suppressing their wants, emotions, and needs. This denial hinders their ability to form responsible relationships. They have difficulty identifying and articulating their requirements and emotions. They may engage in self-sacrifice and feel unworthy if they do not engage in people-pleasing. Inasmuch as the father was unwilling to stand up to his wife in order to shield his children from her control and insults, he fails to set an example of establishing boundaries. Consequently, a son may feel exploited, resentful, and used by women.

Relational concerns

When a boy feels insecure expressing his thoughts and desires to his mother, it appears similarly hazardous in adult relationships. Having been deceived and emotionally abandoned, he fears that his girlfriend will judge him and/or forsake him. Having been entangled with his mother, he also fears being engulfed and subjugated by an intimate partner. As a result, he will avoid intimacy, causing his companion to demand more closeness, which will increase his anxiety and defenses.

Resentment

Even if he remains close to his mother, he may harbor profound animosity toward her if he feels exploited or controlled. Typically, this spreads to other females. Typically, he responds to women with either cooperation, resistance, or rage. Some men are hostile and mistrustful of women. Other males have acquired the ability to be manipulative and passive-aggressive.

They overcompensate, lie, or passively refuse their partner's straightforward requests as if they were their mother's requests. Their aggressive behavior may cause their companion to behave like their mother in the end! Individuals could be dishonest or unfaithful due to resentment and intimacy anxieties, especially if their father was also dishonest or unfaithful.

Repetition

Sons of narcissists are susceptible to developing narcissistic personality disorder. Sons of narcissistic mothers exhibit higher rates of narcissism. This may be due to her tendency to idealize and elevate him rather than compete with him, as she would with a daughter.

Other males may replicate their parental relationship with demanding, dominant, or abusive women. They might date an older woman, a narcissist, an addict, or a person with borderline personality disorder or other mental issues. As with their mother, they may become caregivers to their spouse and find it difficult to depart.

A son must confront his mother's disturbed personality, his wrath at her, and his sadness in order to recover. Eventually, he must show his parents compassion, regardless of whether he respects or loves them. In addition, he must recognize that he deserves affection, establish boundaries with his mother and others, and recognize and communicate his desires and emotions.

Daughters Of Narcissistic Mothers Are Prone To Develop Narcissistic Tendencies

A narcissistic mother who lacks empathy hinders the psychological development of her children.

Through guidance and criticism, a narcissistic mother may attempt to mold her daughter into a version of herself, or her idealized self.

In order to recover from having a narcissistic mother, one must eventually replace their internalized negative parental voice with self-nurturing.

Our mother is the first person we love. She introduces us to the world and to ourselves. She is our security link. We initially learn about ourselves and our circumstances through her interactions. We crave her physical and mental sustenance, her touch, her smile, and her protection. Her empathic reflection of our emotions, aspirations, and requirements reminds us of our identity and value.

A narcissistic mother who lacks empathy hinders the psychological development of her children. Like Narcissus in the Greek myth, she only sees herself in the mirror. There is no line of demarcation separating her from her children, whom she cannot regard as distinct beings deserving of affection. The severity of the symptoms of narcissism that comprise narcissistic personality disorder (NPD) varies, but they always impair a narcissist's ability to parent.

The characteristics and consequences of having a narcissistic mother are as follows. Observe that they are inadvertently repeated in adult abusive relationships, particularly those involving narcissists, because they are familiar—they feel like family.

Lack of limitations

Since girls typically spend more time with their mother and look to her as a role model, some of the effects on daughters are distinct from those on sons.

Narcissistic mothers tend to view their daughters as both threats and extensions of their own personalities. They attempt to mold their daughter into a replica of themselves or their ideal selves through guidance and criticism.

Simultaneously, they project onto their daughter not only undesirable characteristics of themselves, such as self-centeredness, stubbornness, vanity, and coldness, but also despised characteristics of their own mothers. They may favor their son, but in other ways, such as through emotional incest, they may harm him.

Abusive narcissistic behavior

A young girl's burgeoning individuality is impeded by repeated instances of humiliation and control, causing anxiety. She cannot rely on her own thoughts and inclinations and concludes that she is to blame for her mother's anger, not realizing that her mother would never be satisfied.

In extreme cases of mental or physical abuse or neglect, a daughter may feel she has no right to exist, is a burden on her mother, and should have never been born. If they are not also aggressive, spouses of narcissistic women are typically apathetic and do not protect their daughters from maternal abuse.

Some mothers deceive and conceal their abuse. A female is not taught to defend and advocate for herself. Later in life, she may feel defenseless or fail to recognize maltreatment.

noxious shame

Rarely, if ever, does she feel accepted for being herself. She must decide between sacrificing herself and losing her mother's affection; this cycle of self-denial and accommodation is recreated in adult relationships as codependency.

Find a therapist who is familiar with narcissism.

Her authentic personality is rejected by both her mother and herself. The result is internalized humiliation resulting from the belief that her true self is unlovable. How could she be deserving of love if her mother did not accept and adore her? Mothers are supposed to be adored by their children, and vice versa.

A daughter's guilt is exacerbated by her inability to fathom her mother's rage or hatred. She believes it is further evidence of her bad character and that all of her mother's criticisms must be authentic. Her existence is characterized by perpetual striving and a lack of satisfaction. Due to the fact that affection must be earned, her mature relationships may continue a pattern of abandonment.

Emotional unavailability

Emotional solace and proximity in the absence of normal maternal tenderness and caring providers. Narcissistic mothers may meet their daughter's physical needs, but they leave her emotionally desolate. The daughter does not comprehend what is missing, but she longs for the warmth and understanding from her mother that she has witnessed in other mother-daughter relationships with friends or relatives.

She longs for a connection that is either transient or never felt. She does not learn to recognize and value her emotional needs nor how to fulfill them. What remains is a sense of lack and an inability to nurture and console herself. She may try to cover the void in other relationships, but the cycle of emotional unavailability typically repeats itself.

Control

Parents with NPD have impaired vision. The universe is centered on them. When they cannot control and manage their children's needs, emotions, and decisions, they view it as a personal affront deserving of punishment. Typical parenting is "my way or the highway." Some narcissistic mothers focus solely on themselves or their sons, while ignoring or rejecting their daughters.

Other mothers want their daughters to look and be their finest "according to them," but in doing so, they handicap their daughters through criticism and control. These mothers attempt to live vicariously through their daughter, whom they view as an extension of themselves. They want her to dress and act exactly as they do, and to select the same males, interests, and career path.

"For her own good," they can restrict or condemn everything their daughter adores or desires, undermining her ability to think for herself, know what she wants, make her own decisions, and pursue what she desires. Their devotion to their daughter is accompanied by jealously, appreciation, and obedience demands.

Typically, in adult relationships, these females are in dominant relationships or engage in meaningless power struggles.

Competition

When narcissistic mothers believe she is "the prettiest of all" or fear that she is not, they insult their daughter and compete with her for her husband's and sons' affection.

These mothers may not defend their daughter if she is mistreated. They may limit or degrade her partners on the grounds that they are "not good enough," but they still compete for their attention and flirt with them. To be in charge and number one in their daughter's life, parents may invade her privacy and interfere with her relationships with friends and family.

Recovery

Recovering from the trauma of having experienced feelings of rejection and disgrace as a child requires time and effort. Ultimately, it entails codependency recovery. It starts with recognizing and understanding that the demeaning messages and ideas transmitted from mother to daughter are false. The next step is to replace the internalized, negative maternal voice with self-nurturing.

Can A Narcissistic Family Transform?

The point about narcissism is that every person on earth possesses narcissistic characteristics. We are all self-centered in our own ways, and we all desire to feel unique and to be the center of attention (under certain circumstances). Essentially, we are all attempting to distinguish ourselves and create an impact on the world. Therefore, narcissism is NOT a mental disorder. It only becomes a disorder when our narcissistic personality permeates every aspect of our existence. Only when we lack the ability to regulate our emotions and empathy does narcissism manifest as a personality disorder. In this light, narcissism is comparable to a personality disorder, such as borderline personality disorder, or a mood disorder, such as anxiety and melancholy. Can these be controlled, assisted, cured, or even altered? Yes, but it takes a great deal of effort, dedication, patience, and motivation to truly want to follow the advice of professionals in order to get better and manage narcissistic traits. To manage and cope with depression, you must modify various aspects of your life, such as your diet, the way you think, the way you worry, and the way you conduct your life in general. As with any mental or physical health issue, prescription medication will only mask the problem; in order to live a truly satisfying existence, you must put in the effort to overcome it.

To truly transform, narcissists must be comfortable with gaining a deeper emotional understanding of themselves in order to uncover their underlying shame and insecurities. They must learn how to make internal sacrifices, such as giving up the spotlight, being more conscious of their actions so they can place others first, and asking for assistance when they feel too ashamed to do so. To motivate a narcissist to change, they must be confronted with three factors:

Leverage

For the narcissist to seek therapy or even contemplate therapy, there must be some leverage. This could include the fear of losing a loved one, the threat of losing their position or power, or the threat to their social status and reputation.

A therapeutic method

Similarly to how cognitive behavioral therapy (CBT) may be effective for anxiety sufferers and dialectical behavior therapy (DBT) may be effective for those with borderline personality disorder, narcissists must find an effective corrective therapy. A therapy such as schema therapy may be effective for narcissists because it examines the emotional narrative in the brain and concentrates below the intellectual level.

A skilled clinician

A competent therapist is someone who is neither easily attached nor easily persuaded. The ideal therapist for a narcissist is one who can set strong boundaries and does not provoke the narcissist. This would involve the therapist adopting a 'parenting' mentality towards the vulnerable part of the narcissist's psyche, while also holding them accountable for their thoughts and actions. When the 'perfect' psychologist is discovered, the narcissist will be taught how to transform. The modification will appear as follows:

Teaching them the ability to understand their actions and how their actions create negative emotions and thoughts (or vice versa) Teaching the narcissist the consequences of what can happen due to these uncontrollable thoughts and feelings, which in turn gets them to take responsibility for ALL of their actions Allowing the narcissist to believe that they have choices, and based on their choices, they define their outcome (tackling the abusive behavior)

As you can see, assisting a narcissist to transform can be a significant undertaking. However, if a narcissist is in denial about the existence of a problem, they will be unable to acknowledge their faults and would prefer to continue on their current path. The issue with this is that it can be risky to debate and fight with a narcissist, as it can be extremely difficult for the person who suffers because they do not comprehend why they do what they do. If you tell them directly that they are narcissists, their extreme sensitivity to criticism may harm you more than it harms their ego (How to Deal with a Narcissist, 2018).

A Genepool of Narcissists

When we discuss narcissism in the family, we are not referring to a single narcissist. Narcissistic tendencies or characteristics can affect the entire family, because narcissistic parents will inevitably produce narcissistic children. If you have a narcissistic child, someone in the family is likely to make justifications for him or her, which only makes the child more prone to maintaining their traits. This can have a significant impact on every holiday spent with family, turning an afternoon with them into a memorable disaster.

This is what I mean when I state that narcissism impacts the entire family.

The Enabler: This includes a narcissist's spouse, the grandmother of a narcissistic child, or a close sibling. In order to prevent further conflict, the enabler justifies the narcissist's actions.

The Flying Monkey: These family members can be anyone and are typically characterized as those who abuse other family members on the narcissist's behalf. For instance, an adult sister may have severed ties with a narcissistic sibling, and if the parent is the flying monkey, the sister may experience shame and guilt for having done so.

The Scapegoat: This family member has the courage to label the narcissist what they are: an individual with NPD. In lieu of lavishing the narcissist with acclaim and attention, they would rather tell it like it is. Due to their lack of support for the narcissist, the remainder of the family is typically upset with the scapegoat when this type of behavior occurs.

These family traits can make for chaotic holidays, and it may take time for the family as a unit to alter them. Although it is difficult for a single narcissist to change, in order to get the entire family on board and willing to change, certain therapeutic properties and a plan for how things will unfold are required. In addition, it must function for everyone; otherwise, the entire project could fail and narcissistic traits could worsen.

Narcissistic Vacations

On family holidays, there are two possible outcomes: either the narcissist does not attend or they do and the gathering becomes contentious. Holidays such as Christmas, birthdays, Thanksgiving, New Year's, etc., can provoke the rage and perfectionist tantrums of narcissists. Attempting to enjoy the holidays involves and affects not only the narcissist but also the victim, particularly when the narcissist has succeeded in isolating the victim. If you have recently ended a relationship or ceased communicating with a narcissist, you may feel a void during the holidays, particularly if your personality revolved around them, e.g., doing things for them to avoid their wrath, engaging in guilt trips, and playing blame games. Perhaps the most difficult aspect of moving on with your life is figuring out who you are now that you are no longer required to make continuous sacrifices and serve your narcissist.

However, holidays are ideal for getting back on track (if the narcissist is absent). They allow you to reopen up to your family, consume healthily, and reestablish relationships with formerly abundant supportive, positive people. In addition to rebuilding relationships, be sure to take care of yourself during the upcoming holidays. Consider your care in terms of how you would tend to your offspring, regardless of their emotional state. Exercise, get adequate rest, consume plenty of water, show yourself affection, tell yourself uplifting, confidence-building statements, etc. There are additional things you can do during the holiday season to recover from a narcissistic injury, including:

Be tolerant of yourself

You cannot expect to move on immediately, nor can you expect to feel joyful immediately. You may feel relieved until your memories of them remind you of the holiday pleasure you shared with them. Do what makes you joyful while keeping in mind that nothing has to be perfect and nothing has to be a complete failure. If you do not feel like participating in the festivities this year, give yourself more time because you do not have to do anything you do not want to.

2. Accept what was lost so you can restore

What traditions did you observe prior to the narcissist's entrance into your life? Was it observing the holiday lights? Was it donning a costume for Halloween? Was it expressing gratitude by assisting someone in need? You should continue doing whatever it was because the narcissist has not yet spoiled it. If you do not pursue your former interests, you are solely responsible for their demise.

3. Recognize and avoid toxic individuals

Acquaint yourself with problematic individuals and those who are unsupportive of your endeavors, as their presence will only slow down your recovery. Determine which of your acquaintances, family members, and relationships are here for you and which are not. Who wants the best for you and who only uses you to achieve their own ends. The toxic people in your life should be avoided (if possible), while the nontoxic individuals should be sought out for increased interaction.

4. Give, give, give

It is a proved fact that when we give to others, the 'feel-good' endorphin hormones in our brains are released. You can feel good about yourself while giving to others by donating, assisting someone with unloading their shopping, or simply giving them advice. Other ideas include removing litter from the roadways, planting trees, and volunteering at an animal or human shelter.

Because they are so familiar, it can be difficult to appreciate the holidays when the narcissist is absent. As soon as you begin practicing self-awareness and self-love, the days ahead will improve, and you will eventually chuckle at yourself for holding your breath for the abuser. Enjoy the absence of their additional burdens and tension, and remember to be kind to yourself and others.

Narcissists adore holidays, especially because it is simpler for them to take the spotlight and flaunt their superiority or perfection. They enjoy control, conflict, and the spotlight. What better method is there to be boastful and proud during the holidays? I have discussed how holidays can continue without the narcissist, but what if the narcissist is present? Here is what a holiday may look like when narcissists are present at family gatherings.

The curator's handiwork

Holidays provide the narcissist with an opportunity to display their superiority and contend with those around them, from the perfectly decorated Christmas tree to the best New Year's Eve fireworks. If you are invited, they are in charge of everything, but if you are not, don't feel left out because they will post about their success on social media and text you.

The abuse of gift-giving

As narcissists enjoy playing games and having power excursions, they are able to do both during the holidays. During a Christmas event where gifts are exchanged, for instance, the narcissist will not only flaunt their gifts but also inform others that their gifts are superior or will be superior. If you receive a gift from a narcissist, instead of being able to appreciate it, you will be forced to endure the enormous amount of effort they endured in order to obtain that specific gift for you. They will somehow make the gift-giving situation about how they should be thanked for the effort they put into acquiring the item they believed reminded them of you. The narcissist's gift-giving is focused solely on themselves.

The need for management

Have you ever witnessed or participated in the favoritism of one child over another, or if there are no siblings, one individual over everyone else? This is how a narcissist maintains control over a given situation. When they favor one individual but single out another, they invite criticism. This causes conflict because, in many cases, you are truly at the narcissist's residence, so the response is typically "if you don't like it, get out."

The self-centered mother (or father)

There is always a "scapegoat" in the family, as you learned earlier in this chapter. This is not necessarily limited to holiday gatherings. In essence, the person who speaks the truth. However, this scapegoat consistently receives the most difficulty or abuse due to their characteristics. When they disagree with their narcissistic mother's version of the truth — a phenomenon known as gas lighting — all the other children rush to her defense in an attempt to avoid being abused or demeaned. The scapegoat, however, becomes the "black sheep" and is singled out by the mother and the rest of the family as a result of the scapegoat's critical behavior. While the scapegoat is ostracized or singled out, everyone else views and interprets events in the same manner as their mother because this is how they were reared. This is the discarding phase of narcissistic abuse.

While holidays are intended to be enjoyable, they are almost always marred when a narcissist hosts or attends. The best way to cope with a holiday involving narcissistic people is to enjoy the event, tolerate the individual, and then avoid them for as long as possible while making better decisions and building your own life. However, can a narcissistic family transform? As you now know, the answer is yes, but it requires a great deal of effort and labor. To overcome the influence of narcissism, the cycle must be broken.

What Are Narcissism And Narcissistic Personality Disorder?

As one of numerous personality disorders, narcissistic personality disorder is a mental illness characterized by an inflated sense of self-importance, an intense need for excessive admiration and attention, challenging interpersonal relationships, and a lack of empathy for others. Underneath this facade of excessive confidence, however, lies a fragile sense of self-worth that is easily wounded by criticism.

A narcissistic personality disorder causes problems in numerous areas of life, including relationships, employment, education, and finances. People with narcissistic personality disorder may be dissatisfied and dissatisfied when they are denied the privileges or accolades they believe they merit. They may find their relationships unsatisfying, and others may find them unpleasant to be around.

The treatment for narcissistic personality disorder is psychotherapy (talk therapy).

SYMPTOMS

The signs and symptoms and severity of narcissistic personality disorder vary. Those affected by the condition can:

-Have an inflated sense of one's own importance

Have an attitude of entitlement and expect continuous, overwhelming adulation -Expect to be seen as better even without accomplishments that warrant it -Exaggerate accomplishments and skills -Be concerned with illusions of prosperity, power, intelligence, beauty, or the ideal partner -Believe they are exceptional and can only connect with other exceptional individuals -Monopolize conversations and degrade or look down on those they view as inferior -Expect special privileges

-Take advantage of others to get what they want -Have an inability or unwillingness to recognize the needs and emotions of others -Be envious of others and believe others are envious of you

-Behave in an arrogant or haughty manner, coming across as ostentatious, boastful, and pretentious -Demand the best of everything, such as the finest automobile or workplace

Persons with narcissistic personality disorder have difficulty managing what they perceive to be criticism, and they can:

-Have serious interpersonal issues and frequently feel slighted -React with anger or disdain and attempt to denigrate the other person to make oneself look better -Have difficulty regulating emotions and behavior -

Experience major difficulties dealing with stress and adapting to change -Feel depressed and moody because they fall short of perfection -Have hidden feelings of insecurity, shame, vulnerability, and huddling

WHEN TO SEE A PHYSICIAN

Individuals with narcissistic personality disorder may be unwilling to consider that something may be awry, so they are unlikely to seek treatment. If they do seek treatment, it is most likely for depression, substance or alcohol abuse, or another mental health issue. However, perceived insults to self-esteem may make treatment difficult to accept and adhere to.

Consider reaching out to a reputable medical or mental health professional if you recognize characteristics of narcissistic personality disorder in yourself or if you feel overburdened by your grief. Obtaining the appropriate treatment may make your life more fulfilling and joyful.

CAUSES

What causes narcissistic personality disorder is unknown. As with personality development and other mental health disorders, it is likely that the cause of narcissistic personality disorder is complex. There may be a connection between narcissistic personality disorder and the following:

Mismatched parent-child interactions characterized by either excessive adulation or excessive censure that is out of touch with the child's experience.

Genetics inherited characteristics

Neurobiology is the study of the connection between the brain, behavior, and thought.

RISK FACTORS

More men than women suffer from narcissistic personality disorder, and it typically emerges in adolescence or early adulthood. Keep in mind that while some children may exhibit narcissistic behavior, this may be age-appropriate and does not indicate that they will develop narcissistic personality disorder.

Although the cause of narcissistic personality disorder is unknown, some experts believe that overprotective or negligent parenting may play a role in children who are physiologically predisposed. Genetics and neurobiology may also play a role in narcissistic personality disorder development.

COMPLICATIONS

In addition to other disorders, narcissistic personality disorder can be accompanied by the following complications:

Relationship difficulties

Problems at work or school Anxiety and depression

Physical health problems
Drug or alcohol misuse
Suicidal thoughts or actions

PREVENTION

There is no known method of preventing narcissistic personality disorder because its cause is unknown. Nevertheless, it may assist to:

-Get therapy as soon as possible for children's mental health issues - Participate in family counseling to learn healthy ways to communicate or deal with disagreements or emotional turmoil -Attend parenting workshops and seek advice from clinicians or social workers if necessary.

Additional examples and explanations regarding the Symptoms, Causes, Diagnosis, Treatment, and Prevention of narcissism.

The term "narcissism" is commonly used to describe someone who is self-centered. A person who exhibits narcissistic characteristics may suffer from narcissistic personality disorder (NPD).

A personality disorder affects how an individual thinks, behaves, and interacts with others. According to the American Psychiatric Association, "the basic elements of a personality disorder are impairments in personality (self and interpersonal) functioning and the existence of pathological personality traits."

When Does Narcissism Constitute a Personality Disorder?

According to Encyclopedia Britannica, the term "narcissism" is derived from the name of a Greek legendary figure: Narcissus, the son of a deity who fell in love with his own reflection in a spring.

One could argue that everyone has narcissistic tendencies on occasion.

When a person's ability to function and interact with others is impaired, however, such traits are deemed a personality disorder.

Individuals with NPD exhibit excessive confidence, crave attention, and demonstrate little empathy for others. Underneath this veneer of self-assurance, they typically suffer from fragile self-esteem that requires frequent affirmation, followed by feelings of dissatisfaction or inadequacy and an inability to form lasting relationships.

A person with narcissism tends to exhibit the following characteristics in a manner that suggests they believe they are superior:

-Considering oneself to be of the utmost importance -Not being able to accept criticism well -Having an inflated view of one's own potential for success

-Having a desire to be cherished.

If feeling superior or having grandiose beliefs about your place in the world is preventing you from living a joyful life, you should consult a mental health professional about therapy to help you live your best life.

SIGNS AND SYMPTOMS OF NARCISSISM

Not everyone diagnosed with narcissism will exhibit the same symptoms, but narcissism may be characterized by the following emotions and behaviors:

-An inflated sense of self-importance; -a sense of entitlement; -the need for persistent and overwhelming appreciation

Behaving in an arrogant manner that is perceived as ostentatious, boastful, or pretentious -An exaggeration of qualities and accomplishments -A fixation with fantasies of beauty, power, and success -

Feeling superior and desiring interactions with only similarly talented people

-A tendency to dominate conversations

-Looking down on and belittling others - Exploiting others -A reluctance or inability to comprehend the emotions and requirements of others.

-Envy of others -A belief that others are resentful -A determination to acquire the best, in terms of property and position

People with narcissism also have a difficult time accepting criticism, which can cause problems at work and in interpersonal relationships. The following symptoms may hinder their ability to interact with others and function effectively:

-Becoming irritated or impatient if they do not receive special treatment -Feeling readily offended -Reacting with rage or contempt to make oneself appear better

-Difficulty controlling emotions and behavior -Difficulty coping with stress and managing change -Feeling dejected if expectations are not met -Concealed feelings of insecurity, embarrassment, vulnerability, and humiliation

CAUSES AND FACTORS OF NARCISSISM RISK

It is uncertain what causes narcissism exactly. It is presumably a combination of the following variables:

Environmental (early on receiving excessive praise or criticism from parents, for instance) (early on receiving excessive praise or criticism from parents, for example)

Genetic

Neurobiological

In the past, many psychiatrists believed that narcissism was caused by inadequate parental affection and attention. Now we recognize that failing to recognize and assist children in overcoming obstacles may also be detrimental.

Narcissism is more prevalent among men than among women. Typically, it begins during adolescence or early adulthood.

Children may exhibit narcissistic tendencies, but this may be indicative of their age and developmental stage.

Early narcissism does not always predict narcissistic behavior in adulthood.

In reality, it is typical for a very young child to be narcissistic and believe that minor accomplishments are monumental. Despite the fact that it is beneficial for parents to indulge in this age-appropriate narcissism, it becomes developmental imperative in later years to assist older children in recognizing and coping with failure.

www.ingramcontent.com/pod-product-compliance
Lightning Source LLC
Chambersburg PA
CBHW050236120526
44590CB00016B/2110